# Life is Mental:
# Think Thin to Live Thin

An effective, easy to follow
8 week program designed to help you
Think yourself Thin.

## Kelly Stallings

*Think Thin!*
*Kelly*

Life is Mental: Think Thin to Live Thin

Copyright © 2008 by Kelly Stallings

Printed in the United States of America

For information about special discounts for bulk purchases, please contact Kelly Stallings special sales at 713-545-6991or kstallings@lifeismental.com

Cover photo by Bud Tollefsen
Cover design by Jay Michaels

Consult your doctor before starting this or any weight loss program. Individual results will vary.

# Table of Contents

# Introduction

   Changing your thinking and beliefs about your self image and weight loss will create a strong positive foundation for you as you work toward your weight goals. This foundation will assist you in facing challenges and succeeding. If you have experienced past attempts at weight loss that you believe were not successful, then you are ahead of the game! You have great information about yourself to help you identify your triggers or Achilles heal at weight loss and apply the training in this book to push you toward success. You will need to have your caloric intake goals set and your exercise goals set as you begin this 8 week program. You will also need an open mind willing to try new things as you reprogram your thinking to create long lasting success. The benefit you receive from this training will be equal the amount of effort you put into reading the book and applying the principles to your life. If you are completing this book in a group environment (and I hope you are), be open and honest with your group as you move through the weekly chapters. Take time to work through each chapter over the course of each week. Each week you will learn new ideas and strategies to think about and begin applying to your life. Use the time during each week to percolate and practice the ideas and new concepts offered weekly. As your group develops a connection, you will be able to share feedback about one another that may offer significant insights that catapult someone's success.

I would like to be the first to share a significant insight with you. Up to this point, you most likely have not given your weight loss goals all you've got. It is easy to make attempts, get sidetracked by your limiting beliefs and then make excuses. If you are reading this book, you have probably stated your fair share of excuses. This book will help you reach down deep and remove the mental limits that you have placed on yourself. These limits are self imposed negative thoughts and beliefs. You might believe that people in your family are heavy or it is difficult for you to lose weight. Whether these limiting thoughts are your voice or someone else's, it is time they stop and you are freed!

In the movie, *Facing the Giants*, there is a scene where a high school football coach is attempting to show his players that they are not playing to their full ability and believing in themselves. The team has had a poor football record for several years. The coach asks one of the defensive players to stand up and death crawl (crawling on his hands and feet) down the field from one end zone while carrying another player on his back. The coach asks the player how far he can make it. This defense guy says that he can only make it to the 35 yard line while carrying another player and maybe to the 50 with no one his back. The coach says that he believes the player can make it to the 50 yard line with a player on his back and proceeds to blindfold this defense player for the exercise. The player stammers and denies his ability but ultimately positions himself to take the challenge. As the player moves down the field the camera focuses tightly on the coach encouraging him to keep going as the player says he is tired. Soon the camera pans the players on the sidelines standing up and becoming attentive to watch the progress on the field. The coach tells the player to keep going and use up every ounce of will power he has and just keep going. Finally the player falls to his stomach red faced and out of breath apologizing for stopping. The coach takes off his blind fold to reveal the he went the entire length of the field.

This is a great example of the limitations that we set on ourselves and the limitations that others set on us that we accept as true. The blindfold kept the defense player going beyond his own expectations and judgments of his ability. He amazed himself and his team mates. Please think about how you have judged yourself and possibly accepted other people's judgments of you concerning your weight and your ability to lose weight. Picture yourself five years from now. What do you look like in five years? Are you at your perfect weight or are you overweight? This is a significant question for you to really think about. If you picture yourself overweight in your future, do you really believe that you can lose weight? This belief is directly tied to your thinking. Picturing yourself overweight in the future is not thin thinking. You may not have many thin thoughts. You may have a long history of holding limiting beliefs. These limiting beliefs are a choice, not the truth about you. You can choose to change your beliefs and your thinking which will change your life. You have a choice to improve yourself no matter how small the improvements are when you get started. Whether this book helps you achieve your goals in 8 weeks or over the span of 24 weeks, the fact remains that it is your choice to apply this education to your life and start thinking yourself thin. Life is mental; take control of your mind and make something amazing happen!

# Identify Weight Loss Goals

## Set Realistic Goals

Setting realistic goals is an important beginning to successful long term weight loss. Effective goals are 1) specific; 2) attainable; and 3) forgiving (less than perfect). Use the BMI chart included in this book to identify your current BMI status and identify a healthy BMI status and goal weight.

## BMI

Body Mass Index, BMI is a standard of measure to approximate your appropriate body weight based on your height. The formula used to determine your BMI is: your weight in pounds divided by your height in inches squared then multiplied by 703. You can also use the chart on the next page to determine your BMI. Twenty five to thirty is considered overweight. Above 30 is considered obese. The following charts will offer assistance in determining your BMI. There are also several automated calculators online to make this process even easier.

| BMI Ranges | |
|---|---|
| Underweight | < 20 |
| Ideal | 20-25 |
| Overweight | 25-30 |
| Obese | > 30 |

BMI between 20 and 22 is ideal. This indicates healthy body fat. This is the range that most people feel is the most aesthetically attractive. BMI between 22 and 25 is also associated with good health.

# Body Mass Index (BMI)

| BMI — Wgt (lbs) \ Height (in) | 58 | 59 | 60 | 61 | 62 | 63 | 64 | 65 | 66 | 67 | 68 | 69 | 70 | 71 | 72 | 73 | 74 | 75 |
|---|---|---|---|---|---|---|---|---|---|---|---|---|---|---|---|---|---|---|
| | 4'10" | 4'11" | 5'0" | 5'1" | 5'2" | 5'3" | 5'4" | 5'5" | 5'6" | 5'7" | 5'8" | 5'9" | 5'10" | 5'11" | 6'0" | 6'1" | 6'2" | 6'3" |
| 100 | 21 | 20 | 20 | 19 | 18 | 18 | 17 | 17 | 16 | 16 | 15 | 15 | 14 | 14 | 14 | 13 | 13 | 13 |
| 105 | 22 | 21 | 21 | 20 | 19 | 19 | 18 | 18 | 17 | 16 | 16 | 16 | 15 | 15 | 14 | 14 | 14 | 13 |
| 110 | 23 | 22 | 22 | 21 | 20 | 20 | 19 | 18 | 18 | 17 | 17 | 16 | 16 | 15 | 15 | 15 | 14 | 14 |
| 115 | 24 | 23 | 23 | 22 | 21 | 20 | 20 | 19 | 19 | 18 | 18 | 17 | 17 | 16 | 16 | 15 | 15 | 14 |
| 120 | 25 | 24 | 23 | 23 | 22 | 21 | 21 | 20 | 19 | 19 | 18 | 18 | 17 | 17 | 16 | 16 | 15 | 15 |
| 125 | 26 | 25 | 24 | 24 | 23 | 22 | 22 | 21 | 20 | 20 | 19 | 18 | 18 | 17 | 17 | 17 | 16 | 16 |
| 130 | 27 | 26 | 25 | 25 | 24 | 23 | 22 | 22 | 21 | 20 | 20 | 19 | 19 | 18 | 18 | 17 | 17 | 16 |
| 135 | 28 | 27 | 26 | 26 | 25 | 24 | 23 | 23 | 22 | 21 | 21 | 20 | 19 | 19 | 18 | 18 | 17 | 17 |
| 140 | 29 | 28 | 27 | 27 | 26 | 25 | 24 | 23 | 23 | 22 | 21 | 21 | 20 | 20 | 19 | 19 | 18 | 18 |
| 145 | 30 | 29 | 28 | 27 | 27 | 26 | 25 | 24 | 23 | 23 | 22 | 21 | 21 | 20 | 20 | 19 | 19 | 18 |
| 150 | 31 | 30 | 29 | 28 | 27 | 27 | 26 | 25 | 24 | 24 | 23 | 22 | 22 | 21 | 20 | 20 | 19 | 19 |
| 155 | 32 | 31 | 30 | 29 | 28 | 28 | 27 | 26 | 25 | 24 | 24 | 23 | 22 | 22 | 21 | 20 | 20 | 19 |
| 160 | 34 | 32 | 31 | 30 | 29 | 28 | 28 | 27 | 26 | 25 | 24 | 24 | 23 | 22 | 22 | 21 | 21 | 20 |
| 165 | 35 | 33 | 32 | 31 | 30 | 29 | 28 | 28 | 27 | 26 | 25 | 24 | 24 | 23 | 22 | 23 | 21 | 21 |
| 170 | 36 | 34 | 33 | 32 | 31 | 30 | 29 | 28 | 27 | 27 | 26 | 25 | 24 | 24 | 23 | 22 | 22 | 21 |
| 175 | 37 | 35 | 34 | 33 | 32 | 31 | 30 | 29 | 28 | 27 | 27 | 26 | 25 | 24 | 24 | 23 | 23 | 22 |
| 180 | 38 | 36 | 35 | 34 | 33 | 32 | 31 | 30 | 29 | 28 | 27 | 27 | 26 | 25 | 24 | 24 | 23 | 23 |
| 185 | 39 | 37 | 36 | 35 | 34 | 33 | 32 | 31 | 30 | 29 | 28 | 27 | 27 | 26 | 25 | 24 | 24 | 23 |
| 190 | 40 | 38 | 37 | 36 | 35 | 34 | 33 | 32 | 31 | 30 | 29 | 28 | 27 | 27 | 26 | 25 | 24 | 24 |
| 195 | 41 | 39 | 38 | 37 | 36 | 35 | 34 | 33 | 32 | 31 | 30 | 29 | 28 | 27 | 27 | 26 | 25 | 24 |
| 200 | 42 | 40 | 39 | 38 | 37 | 36 | 34 | 33 | 32 | 31 | 30 | 30 | 29 | 28 | 27 | 26 | 26 | 25 |
| 205 | 43 | 41 | 40 | 39 | 38 | 36 | 35 | 34 | 33 | 32 | 31 | 30 | 29 | 29 | 28 | 27 | 26 | 26 |
| 210 | 44 | 43 | 41 | 40 | 38 | 37 | 36 | 35 | 34 | 33 | 32 | 31 | 30 | 29 | 29 | 28 | 27 | 26 |
| 215 | 45 | 44 | 42 | 41 | 39 | 38 | 37 | 36 | 35 | 34 | 33 | 32 | 31 | 30 | 29 | 28 | 28 | 27 |
| 220 | 46 | 45 | 43 | 42 | 40 | 39 | 38 | 37 | 36 | 35 | 34 | 33 | 32 | 31 | 30 | 29 | 28 | 28 |
| 225 | 47 | 45 | 44 | 43 | 41 | 40 | 39 | 38 | 36 | 35 | 34 | 33 | 32 | 31 | 31 | 30 | 29 | 28 |
| 230 | 48 | 47 | 45 | 44 | 42 | 41 | 40 | 38 | 37 | 36 | 35 | 34 | 33 | 32 | 31 | 30 | 30 | 29 |
| 235 | 49 | 48 | 46 | 44 | 43 | 42 | 40 | 39 | 38 | 37 | 36 | 35 | 34 | 33 | 32 | 31 | 30 | 29 |
| 240 | 50 | 49 | 47 | 45 | 44 | 43 | 41 | 40 | 39 | 38 | 37 | 36 | 35 | 34 | 33 | 32 | 31 | 30 |
| 245 | 51 | 50 | 48 | 46 | 45 | 43 | 42 | 41 | 40 | 38 | 37 | 36 | 35 | 34 | 34 | 33 | 32 | 31 |
| 250 | 52 | 51 | 49 | 47 | 46 | 44 | 43 | 42 | 40 | 39 | 38 | 37 | 36 | 35 | 34 | 33 | 32 | 31 |
| 255 | 53 | 52 | 50 | 48 | 47 | 45 | 44 | 43 | 41 | 40 | 39 | 38 | 37 | 36 | 35 | 34 | 33 | 32 |
| 260 | 54 | 53 | 51 | 49 | 48 | 46 | 45 | 43 | 42 | 41 | 40 | 38 | 37 | 36 | 35 | 34 | 33 | 33 |
| 265 | 55 | 54 | 52 | 50 | 49 | 47 | 46 | 44 | 43 | 42 | 40 | 39 | 38 | 37 | 36 | 35 | 34 | 33 |
| 270 | 56 | 55 | 53 | 51 | 49 | 48 | 46 | 45 | 44 | 42 | 41 | 40 | 39 | 38 | 37 | 36 | 35 | 34 |
| 275 | 58 | 56 | 54 | 52 | 50 | 49 | | | | | | | | | | | | |

# Weekly Check In

Each week you will weigh in and measure your arm, stomach and thigh. This variety of data is important to help you identify how to effectively track your progress. Everyone loses weight differently. Some people lose pounds and their weight will drop without effort. Other people strengthen and tone and lose inches instead of pounds. Since muscle weighs more than fat, a size 8 strengthened body will weigh more than a size 8 weak body. Do not let yourself get attached or emotional about your weekly numbers. The numbers are not as accurate a measurement as compared to how you physically feel and how your clothes fit you. These numbers are simply the easiest way to track progress in this book.

As you complete your measurements, notice how your clothes are fitting you. You might choose a specific pair of pants that fit you snuggly to try on at each weekly check in. Using the same pair of pants will help you really see the changes in your body as you lose weight by putting these on each week. Regardless of your measurements, loose pants will make you feel great and keep you motivated. Your weight is just a number; your physical appearance is what you look at to evaluate your true progress.

Do not compare your progress with the other members in the group. Comparing is poisonous to your attitude. Everyone is unique and will lose weight differently. Keep a constant focus on all the positives for every check in. ALL progress is positive progress. You may have a week where your progress is not actual inches or pounds, but learning some significant insight into your personality that will assist your long term weight loss. If you stay committed to your program, you WILL reach your weight goal in the length of time necessary for your body.

---

**Weekly Check In**

Date:

Current Weight:            Goal Weight:

Measurements:

Arm_____     Stomach_____     Thigh_____

BMI:                Goal BMI:

---

# Start Thinking Thin

> You can be anything you want to be, if only you believe with
> sufficient conviction and act in accordance with your faith;
> for whatever the mind can conceive and believe,
> the mind can achieve.
> **Napoleon Hill**
> *Author of Think and Grow Rich*

This book is an opportunity to achieve the body size that is right for you. It is designed to help you think thin. You can pick it up and put it down as many times as needed. The information offered here is always here for you. It is here to get you started, here to help you reach your goals, and here to keep you maintaining your best self. The best is yet to come. You will be victorious achieving your goals this time. Conceive your potential on the inside and create it on the outside. You will need to do your part to create your potential. Following through with your plan, keep working your plan if you slip, and minding your mind is your charge. Do not depend on other people, this is all about you.

You do not need others to believe in your dream to make it a success. Tell yourself, 'I am equipped with what I need to be successful.' At this moment, you have within you what you need to reach your goals. When I was young girl, my mother put a magnate on the refrigerator that said 'If you think you can...YOU CAN!' I read this magnate every time that I went to or by our refrigerator. Those words made an impression on my mind. I believed this phrase and constantly had positive thoughts about my abilities. When I moved out of my parent's home, I took the magnate with me for my refrigerator and now my kids read it (well, at least they see it) every time they go to the refrigerator. I grew up believing that I could decide to do or be anything I chose. Because of this, I view mistakes or roadblocks as temporary setbacks that offer me profound education of some sort to help me reach my goals. Viewing life challenges as learning experiences allows you to keep a more positive attitude and pull out of personal pity parties quickly. It is hard to feel bad if you believe that you just learned something that will help you become successful in the future. Let me share that idea again, temporary setbacks are educational experiences that catapult me toward my goals. You may have tried to lose weight in the past; those were learning experiences that will allow you to go farther this time. You will reach your goals.

**Commitment versus Interest**

There is a big difference between having an interest in losing weight and being committed to losing weight. While you may have some modest success with an interest, you will need a true commitment to achieve your weight loss goals and maintain the loss over time. If you have any reservations, let your interest get you started. Your immediate changes may energize you and grow your interest to a commitment.

I have a friend who wanted to lose weight without changing anything in her lifestyle. This may be similar to you. I am sure that you know long term weight loss is not a magical experience that will occur and sustain without a lifestyle change from your current habits. She started taking a particular natural weight loss product program and saw some modest results. She felt more energy and her mood appeared elevated. These modest results grew her interest and

she started making positive lifestyle changes to grow
her commitment and increase her weight loss.  Let this
inspire you to act on your desires and grow your commitment stronger every day.
　　If you are clear from the beginning about
whether you are committed or interested, you will be
able to enjoy the successes that you experience either
way.  It is will be easy for you to pick up the plan and
keep moving forward in the future if you find that you
are currently more interested than committed.  The
beauty of using a cognitive plan to lose weight is that
you can constantly be improving your thoughts which
will directly relate back to your motivation.  The longer
you keep thinking thin, the stronger your commitment
will grow in the other areas of your life necessary for
weight loss.  Thinking thin is your answer to a healthier thinner you!

### What is your Motivation?

　　Motivation to lose weight can develop from many
sources in our lives.  You may have a medical issue
that requires you to lose weight to sustain better health
and possibly avoid more critical medical issues.  You
may be significantly overweight and feel embarrassed
and/or self conscious in social situations.  You may be
just slightly over a healthy BMI index and want to lose
weight to look better and feel better.  You may want to
look thin in your size 6 swim suit at the beach this
summer.  These reasons will directly relate to your
weight loss goals.  Whatever your reason, you need to
address the thoughts and attitudes that you hold about
yourself both physically and emotionally.  This cognitive process that is constantly running in your mind
can lead you to long term successful weight loss or
short term losses and gains (yo-yo).  What are your

common thoughts about your physical image? Are you self critical and a perfectionist? Do you hold yourself to a higher standard than you hold others around you? Are you a pessimist that does not believe that you can achieve long term success in weight loss? If your thoughts are negative, they will surely lead you to self sabotage at some point on your journey. This is why you need to think yourself thin.

Thinking yourself thin will help you adopt the common thoughts and beliefs held by thin people. Thin thoughts will assist you in developing a positive self appreciation and encourage you to enjoy the journey of weight loss by viewing food in a whole new light. Thin thoughts will allow you to make some poor choices in diet and exercise along the way and get back on track. Thin thoughts will eliminate the harsh judgments that you hold for yourself and help you appreciate your assets.

This is probably not the first time that you have had an interest in weight loss. Successful long term weight loss will require a commitment on your part to make the necessary changes to achieve your goals. While this book will walk you through making mental changes, you will need to modify your physical activity and caloric intake. Consult your medical doctor before starting any new calorie program and physical activity.

As you get started with your physical and caloric regime, let's focus on your thoughts and get them aligned with your goals for long term success!

## Reasons for Weight Loss

Thinking yourself thin starts with identifying the reasons to lose weight. These are most likely very compelling reasons directly associated with your moti-vation to lose weight. Take a moment to think about the different reasons that you want to lose weight. You may not feel comfortable with the fit of your clothes or the physical limitations you experience. You may have medical concerns with your weight. Whatever the reasons, you need to be clear on them now as you get started with this program. Clarifying your reasons for weight loss will act as a motivator during the program. These reasons will also give you a way to determine progress. As these reasons become positive realities in your life, you will be supercharged toward your ultimate weight goals.

The Reasons for Weight Loss exercise at the end of this chapter directs you to list your reasons to lose weight in detail. Write all of the reasons for you to lose weight that you can identify. Be as detailed as you can for each reason. Phrase each item with the words, "I am" as if this reason has already been fulfilled. This will indicate to your mind that this is a reason that you have achieved. You are acting 'as if' it has already happened. Acting 'as if' is a powerful way to reprogram your thinking which leads to goal achievement. Truly see and believe your success in reaching your goals and you will begin to take action to make this a reality. An example for this exercise is, 'I am wearing a size 8 swim suit and I feel comfortable at the beach with my family.' The more specific detail that you describe and connect with emotion, the more powerful this list will become for you. Use this list to effectively help you through the tough moments on your weight loss journey. You will be reading and rereading this list to keep you mindful of your goals and desires. Every time you read this list and feel the positive emotion of your upcoming new physique, you will feel renewed and strong in the face of food cravings or a plateau in your weight loss.

Use this detailed list to rewrite your top Reasons for Weight Loss on a small card that you can keep with you at all times. Keep it in your wallet so that you will always have access to it for motivation and strength. Transcribe this list onto several small cards that can be posted around home and work environment. Add the list as a screen saver on your computer. Read this list thoughtfully three times a day allowing yourself to visualize your goals as achieved and feel the emotions that these reasons elicit. See and feel yourself being confident with your new body size.

> Whether you think you can or you think you can't,
> you are probably right.
> **Henry Ford**

## Daily Food Journal

Your Daily Food Journal (DFJ) will be an easy form to complete as you go through the day or at the end of the day. The DFJ form can be found in the appendix of the workbook. A blank template is also included for use beyond this 8 week program for more aggressive goals and maintenance. The DFJ will offer you a wealth of information to help you make mental changes that will create significant results in your life. Use the DFJ to make notes on what you eat during the day and when you eat it. List the food items in the order from morning to evening. Include reason for eating, like hungry, bored, or sad. These reasons for eating are important information. If you notice that every evening you eat a late snack because you are bored, you can modify your activity level to avoid this unnecessary snack and calories. These reasons will indicate unnecessary eating that you can strategically avoid, it will help you identify if there is a certain time of day or certain foods that challenge your weight loss goals. For example, do you stop by a coffee shop in the afternoon for a coffee boost and feel tempted to eat a sweet at the same time? Use this insight to create the solution to your challenge. After identifying any regular challenges, you can create a plan of action to avoid the challenge. This book will offer many options for overcoming your challenges.

Notice the additional sections for exercise and positivity entries. Each day you can make note of the physical activity and positive affirmations that you complete. The physical activity entries will help you give yourself credit for not only planned, but spontaneous exercise. Spontaneous exercise is any physical activity that occurs in the normal course of your day. Walking from your car to your office is spontaneous exercise. You may find that your spontaneous exercise grows simply by noting it. Spontaneous exercise leads to more daily activity and a healthier lifestyle. Give yourself credit for every activity that you make note of that moves you closer to your goals. The positivity entries will offer you motivation to keep going through challenging moments. The uses of these entries will be described in more detail later in this workbook.

Make the DFJ a positive experience that you quickly complete. As you see the numerous benefits from using this journal, you will be excited to complete the entries daily so that you can identify strategies that will assist your life long success with maintaining your goal weight.

## My Reasons for Weight Loss

List all of the reasons that you want to lose weight. Start each item with the words 'I am' and use present tense indicating that the reason is already achieved. Be specific and include feeling words with your descriptions. This detail will assist you in later defining themes for motivating you during the challenging moments of your weight loss journey. Be open about the emotions that you will feel with weight loss. The more detail you incorporate with emotions, the easier it will be to visualize and achieve these goals.

Here are some questions to get you thinking...
* How will you feel about yourself when you trim down?
* How will weight loss affect your lifestyle and activity level?
* Will your relationships change as you achieve a healthy weight?
* Will your activity regimen change as a result of weight loss?

1.
2.
3.
4.
5.
6.
7.
8.
9.
10.

Copy the top few reasons for weight loss on to several 3X5 cards. Post the cards around your home and in your car to read multiple times daily. Cut one of the cards in half to fit in your wallet for access at any time. These cards will help you keep your mind on your goals and create thin thinking.

## Plan for Week 1

1) Post your Reasons for Weight Loss cards around your home where you will read the card multiple times daily. Your bathroom mirror, your bedside table, your pantry door, your refrigerator, your desk, and your car dashboard are all good places to post cards. Transfer these reasons to your computer as a screen saver. Keep a small copy in your wallet so that you have this motivation boost at all times.

2) Read your Reasons for Weight Loss before each of your meals and before bedtime. Read through the list slowly and focus on the visual and the emotion of each reason. This is a great long term technique to keep you motivated and focused on your goals especially when you feel your motivation waning and temptation to veer from your program.

3) Track your food intake and exercise on your Daily Food Journal.

Weekly Check In

Date:

Current Weight: Goal Weight:

Measurements:

Arm_____ Stomach_____ Thigh_____

BMI: Goal BMI:

# Positivity is Thin Thinking

Every negative event contains within it
the seed of an equal or greater benefit.

**Napoleon Hill**
*Author of Think and Grow Rich*

## Positivity

Following a meal plan and exercise regime is
pretty straightforward. There are some specific meas-
urable objectives that you follow to achieve success
with each activity. The thoughts that you allow yourself to focus on can make following these directives a
breeze or a challenge. Your motivated thoughts of
thinness, enjoying the feeling of exercise, etc., can
make your weight loss move forward effortlessly. On
the other hand, thoughts that focus on how unfair life
is that you cannot eat fried foods everyday will defi-
nitely slow the process. Essentially your mind can
work for you or against you with your consent.

In a New England Journal of Medicine study,
physicians studying the effect of arthroscopic knee
surgery assigned 180 military veterans to one of three
surgical procedures: scraping out the knee joint, wash-
ing out the joint, or doing nothing. (July 2002) During
the 'sham' procedure, doctors anesthetized the patients,
made incisions in the knee as if to insert their surgical
instruments, and pretended to operate. Two years
after surgery, patients in all groups reported the same
amount of relief from pain and swelling as those who
had received actual treatments. The patients in the
'sham' procedure group expected the 'surgery' to improve the knee and it did. Life events teach our brain
what to expect. We expect certain events and we often

achieve or develop exactly what we expect. What are
your expectations? Are they cynical or optimistic? Do
you expect to have weight problems? Do you have
overweight family members that cause you to believe
that you will also be overweight?

## Teaching your Mind to Work for You

The majority of the population defaults to negative or limiting thoughts. It is important to identify
these negative limiting thoughts and reverse them. An
example of a negative thought might be, 'I have tried
weight loss in the past and was not successful. It
probably will not work this time either.' Positive
statements that you create to reverse these negative
thoughts will move you toward your goals. These are
thin thoughts. A positive thin thought for the previous
example might be, 'All of my past attempts at weight
loss have taught me something about myself. This
time I will be successful.' Once you create your new
positive statement or belief, you will need to implant it
into your subconscious mind. This reprogramming is
done by constant repetition several times each day for a
minimum of 30 days.

Keeping a positive mental attitude allows you
believe and embrace your weight loss goals. Positive
thoughts will keep you moving forward toward your
goals in the face of shortfalls or stressful days. When
you hit a plateau in your weight loss, and you will
because it is normal part of the process, positive thinking will keep you on track through the experience. You
will be able to remind yourself that plateauing is
normal. Positive thoughts will keep you in the right
frame of mind to review your options of waiting it out,
restricting some of your calories, or increasing your
physical activity.

Positivity is a mindset. Anyone can enjoy it. If it seems hokey, then you most likely hold a lot of negative thinking causing you to judge the concept. I encourage you to put aside any judgments and give this a genuine effort. You have nothing to lose by giving this concept a genuine effort. Start by listening to your thoughts and converting negative thoughts to positive ones. This skill may take ongoing effort and possibly a positivity buddy to make positivity a default in your brain.

Quickly identify any negative or limiting thoughts that immediately enter your mind as related to weight loss. The negative thoughts that quickly come to your mind about your weight loss goals are probably the strongest. List these thoughts and then rewrite them as a positive. This initial list is an exercise to start this process for you. In the next section of this chapter, you will be instructed to use your DFJ to continue identifying your negative thinking. List only the positive version of your negative thought on your DFJ. This allows you to focus on the positive thought that you are programming.

*Weight Loss Thoughts:*

Negative
**Positive**

Negative
**Positive**

Negative
**Positive**

Negative
**Positive**

Negative
**Positive**

Stay mindful of your thoughts and continue this process during the course of this program. The more comprehensive your list, the more positivity you will be creating for yourself. Repetitious reading of your positive thoughts will over time change your default mental settings into more positive thin thoughts. Post or write the strongest thoughts in positive form in areas of your life that will allow you to read them daily for the next 30 days.

**Positivity Journal**

There is a vehicle repair shop in my hometown that always puts catchy little phrases on their marquis. Recently, the marquis read 'Don't add up your troubles, Count your Blessings.' This is an important directive for life. Creating a positivity journal allows you to count your blessings and focus on the positive aspects of your life. You will naturally feel better and grow more positives in your life if you keep track of these as closely as you have kept track of the negatives in your life.

Use this list of newly created positive statements to create the beginning of your Positivity Journal. Your positivity journal is embedded into your Daily Food Journal making your DFJ multipurpose. Add positive thoughts to your DFJ as you identify and create them from negative thoughts. Simply jot down your positive thoughts during the day. These positivity statements will boost your motivation at that moment and when you reread past entries.

As you make note of your negative thoughts and convert them to positive statements, you will begin to identify some positive thoughts that are very significant to your long term goals. These might be thoughts that you think about daily or in specific situations. The positive thoughts that you identify to be the most important to you at the top of your list make great motivating cards to use with your Reasons for Weight Loss Card. For example, you might slip on your food choices by eating a poor food choice and proceed to think negative thoughts about yourself catastrophizing your weight loss success. This thought will need to be reprogrammed with a positive thin thought. Your positive thin thought, "a slip does not sabotage my diet because I will slightly modify food choices over the next two days and get back on track," will prove to be a very important positive thought to program as a new default setting. This is a great example of a positive thin thought to read daily.

Write the significant and powerful positive statements that you want to program as your default setting on the cards similar to your Reasons for Weight Loss. Write them on your bathroom mirror. Write them on the shower door with your finger and every time you take a hot shower, the steam will reveal your positive thought. Get creative to get your attention! Incorporate them into your reading regime for a minimum of 30 days.

## Dress for Positivity

Use the cool silicone 'Think Thin' band or a rubber band to make a significant impact on your positivity. Place the band on your right wrist when you get up in the morning. This is an effective strategy because positivity will support thinking and living thin. At any time that you have a negative thought, move the band to the opposite wrist and restate/rethink the negative as a positive. If you eat a donut and start berating yourself, move the band and tell yourself that eating a donut is not the end of the thin you. This reminder band will help you keep a positive thin thinking mindset. The goal is to wear the band for 30 days straight without moving it the opposite wrist at any time during the day. Every time you move the band, you start at day one again. This is a significant time commitment to this exercise. The reason is to truly create and repetitively reinforce a new habit. It took you quite a while to create and repeatedly reinforce the bad habit of negative thinking or negative self talk; it will certainly take a while to replace that bad habit with a good one.

You may be moving the bracelet between wrists several times as you begin using this technique. This is normal. Make sure that you are converting your negative thought into a positive one that can be used in your positivity journal as you move your bracelet. Repeatedly reinforcing this negative to positive conversion will create a habit for you that will serve your future. When you have worn your band on the same hand without moving it for 30 days, you will have created a new habit of positive thinking that allows you to have more mental flexibility and self acceptance. You will be thinking thin.

### Physical Activity

Physical Activity is crucial to healthy living. Activity keeps our bodies flexible and healthy. This is the week to identify your exercise options if you have not already started exercising. There are a variety of physical activities that a person can do to burn calories. It is important that you get the approval of your medical doctor before doing anything strenuous.

There are two types of exercise: planned and spontaneous. The planned exercise is represented by organized sports, gym membership, martial arts classes, etc. This is the activity that you will plan into your schedule on a weekly basis. Spontaneous exercise is just that, spontaneous. Taking the stairs instead of the elevator or parking farther away from the door of a building to add to your walk from the car are examples of spontaneous exercise. There are multiple opportunities daily for spontaneous exercise. Once you begin looking for

*"Visiting your health club's website is a start, but I'd prefer you actually go there and exercise."*

these opportunities or creating them in your life, you are on your way to easy daily activity.

According to the National Institute of Health, regular physical activity is important to your overall health and fitness. It helps you control body weight by increasing the calories you expend each day. NIH recommends that you are physically active at moderate intensity for at least 30 minutes most days of the week. Increasing the intensity or the amount of time that you are physically active can have greater health benefits for controlling body weight. Calories consumed from foods must be balanced by the calories used in daily activities.    You can see that any regular activity to get your heart rate elevated is beneficial to your weight loss. A great way to get you started is to use a pedometer. Use a pedometer to track how many steps you take each day during any average day. You are tracking your spontaneous exercise. The first time you use the pedometer gives you a baseline. Keep the pedometer on your body daily and increase the number of steps you take each day. Park farther from the door or take the stairs instead of the elevator to increase your steps. Easy right? This is easy and effective. As you continue to increase your steps, you will feel more energetic and develop more motivation to increase your physical activity to more than simply walking.

## Reward Success

It is important to reward your successes regularly no matter how small the achievement. Give yourself kudos for a job well done to keep your focus on the positive progress that you are making toward your goals. By focusing on the positive, you are distracting yourself from the natural human tendency of keeping tabs on all of your shortcomings which serves only to get you off track and feel negative. Rewarding yourself works. Everyone wants to be acknowledged for successes. The positive acknowledgment is effective whether it comes from yourself or others.

Identify something you would like to reward for completion. This may be something that you need some encouragement to complete like your exercise regime. Maybe a small success with your exercise like completing your planned exercise for the week or completing your DFJ each day of the week can be celebrated to encourage you toward completion. Keep these celebrations relational to the size of the success. For example, if you reach your exercise goals for the week you may treat yourself to a massage, a good movie or a hot bath with essential oils for relaxation. Rewards can be items that you buy for yourself, services that you purchase, or special time for activities that you enjoy without interruption. Rewards need to be timely to keep you motivated to continue toward more rewards. If you establish a weekly reward for something, make sure you enjoy your reward each week if you meet your goal. Choose something that you enjoy experiencing or a material reward that you would enjoy having.

DO NOT use food as a reward. Food as a reward creates a psychological struggle with food. Food as a reward rationalizes poor food choices. If you want a food that does not fit your food plan, then choose to eat it in moderation. If you choose to eat a certain food, take responsibility for eating the food. Eating poor food choices in moderation keeps you from feeling deprived. Take responsibility and control of your eating.

Need some ideas for rewards?

Items for Purchase:
- New book with positive theme
- CD of upbeat or relaxation music
- New article of clothing
- Small item for home or office
- Special dishes purchased one at a time

Services:
- Massage
- Manicure/pedicure
- Facial
- Yoga session

Special Self Treatment:
- Afternoon nap
- Hot soaking bath
- Bike ride
- Special reading time

## Plan for Week 2

1) Complete the List of Negative Thoughts and re-write them as Positive Thoughts. This list is the beginning of your Positivity Journal. Continue adding positive thoughts that you create and use on your DFJ

2) Add positive statements for reprogramming cards to your Reasons for Weight Loss cards. Read your Reasons for Weight Loss/Positive reprogramming cards daily before each meal and for a motivation boost. Keep a small copy in your wallet so that you have this motivation boost at all times to use to distract from cravings. After rereading the cards several times, just the memory that the card is in your wallet can have a positive effect on your mood between readings.

3) Track your food intake on your Daily Food Journal (DFJ).

4) Identify your exercise regimen. Make certain that the plan is consistent regardless of the activity. Choose an activity that you enjoy to make compliance easier. Identify both planned and spontaneous physical activity. Enter this activity on your DFJ.

5) Use a pedometer to track the number of steps you take each day. Increase the number of steps each day. Record your daily steps on your DFJ.

6) Identify behaviors that you would like to reward and identify a weekly reward for yourself.

## Weekly Check In

Date:

Current Weight:            Goal Weight:

Measurements:

Arm_____     Stomach_____     Thigh_____

BMI:                Goal BMI:

# Brain - Body Connection

> And be not conformed to this world: but be ye transformed
> by the renewing of your mind. Romans 12:2

## Hunger

Hunger is a true lack of food in your stomach.
This is a feeling that will not go away with time.
Typically time makes it stronger. Missing a meal
causes hunger. If you have eaten a meal and still feel
hungry, this is typically a craving not hunger. Hunger
is normal. Feeling hungry does not mean that you
need to eat immediately; however, do not let yourself
get so hungry that you feel faint or weak. If you are
slightly becoming hungry, tell yourself that your next
regular meal or snack will be soon and you will eat at
that time. Distract yourself until that time. Thin
thinking adapts to hunger by using distracting
thoughts until it is time to eat.

If you are really hungry with your stomach
growling, feed yourself. As you identify true hunger,
eat. This may be different that what you expected to
read. Thin people feed themselves when they feel
hungry. Thin people do not eat to excess; they feed
their hunger and stop when they feel full. The key is to
stop when you feel full. Later in this chapter you will
be taught how to identify feeling full. Your body will
tell you when to quit eating. Starting today, eat when
you are truly physically hungry and stop eating when
you feel full.

Depriving your body of food makes your body
think you are starving and it starts holding onto fat.
This is not good. Starving yourself also sets up mental
stress. You feel hungry and then keep telling yourself

not to eat until you get so hungry that you binge. After the binge, you feel guilty and believe that you need to starve yourself again to make up for the binge. You might find yourself focused on when and what you can eat. Your whole life becomes centered around food and eating instead of living and enjoying your life. This is seriously flawed thinking that creates an unhealthy weight cycle. Starving yourself also significantly affects your mood.

If you are someone who does not like to feel hunger or if you view hunger as the immediate need to eat, learn to tolerate some feelings of hunger. Initial thoughts that you may be getting hungry are normal and not a signal to stop and eat. Your body is just beginning to signal. Hunger is not an emergency. With that said, do not let yourself get to the point of hunger that you are faint or lightheaded. If you wait too long to eat, you will most times eat too much because you will eat too fast. Since hunger grows in stages, the goal is to eat when you feel hungry beyond the initial thoughts of hunger and before you reach the weak, light headed stage. Keeping yourself fed will reduce overeating and level your mood. You will feel better and allow your body to regulate the weight down. This is going to be an important skill to master for long term success with your weight.

This week, focus on feeding your body and stopping when you are full. Do this with whatever food your body desires. Eat what you want when you are truly hungry and stop eating when you feel full. This will make you feel happy and satisfied. When you restrict a desired food in your diet, you will most times start craving this food because it is restricted. You might start fixating on the food making the craving worse. By allowing yourself to eat whatever you desire, you take away cravings. Do not be concerned about what foods you are eating this week. Be concerned and focused on stopping when you begin to feel full. As you master this skill, you will naturally want to eat healthier foods to see results faster.

## Conscious Eating

When was the last time you remember truly enjoying the food you ate? If you are like many Americans, you rush through your meal or multitask while you eat. You may have the television going, using your laptop or reading while you eat. This is unconscious eating. Your attention is focused on these other tasks and not on eating. Eating consciously is very important. Focusing your attention on your food allows you to enjoy your food and notice your 'Full Signal' to stop eating. Unconscious eating leads to overeating. You are so focused on your environment that you do not notice your full signal to stop eating. From today forward, eat slowly while seated and savor your food to eat consciously.

No more eating on the run. You are less likely to keep track of what you are eating if you are eating while moving around with activity. For some reason many people believe the mini donut they eat while getting dressed in the morning does not count as calorie intake. Wrong! Give yourself the rule of sitting down to eat EVERYTHING. As you sit, eat slowly and pay attention to every texture and taste. Put your fork or spoon down after every mouthful of food. Putting utensils down is very important to do when learning to eat consciously. DO NOT skip this step! Put your utensils down between every bite. Chew your food 15 to 20 times before swallowing. Savor your food every time you sit down to eat. By placing your fork or spoon

down between each bite, you will be successful at
eating slowly.

Use the savor your food exercise to practice savoring your food. Eating slowly allows your stomach to
register to your brain that you are getting full so that
you do not overeat. It takes 10-20 minutes for your
brain to register that your stomach is full. If you eat
quickly, you can easily train yourself to overeat and
become accustomed to an overly full feeling. Speed
eating is common in our fast paced, clean your plate
culture.

You should be able to comfortably take a brisk
walk after finishing a meal. If you cannot imagine
walking after a meal, chances are that you have eaten
too much. This technique also gives you a sense of
enjoyment and satisfaction for the food you eat. This
new rule will really affect highly active people. You
may decide not to eat that mini donut if you have to sit
down and slow down.

## Savor Your Food Exercise

Eating slowly and savoring your food may be a
foreign concept for you. This exercise will help you
slow down and enjoy your food. Complete this exercise
to teach you to savor your food. Use a small chocolate
or raisin for this exercise. Place the chocolate or raisin
in your mouth on your tongue. Do no chew. Notice the
taste of the chocolate and the texture on your tongue.
Are your taste buds reacting to the chocolate? Notice
this feeling. After several minutes of this experience,
slowly chew the chocolate and focus on the taste and
texture as you chew. After 10-15 chews, swallow and
notice the chocolate going down your throat. This
entire experience should take at least 5 minutes. What
was this experience like for you? Did you notice any-

thing new about eating the chocolate that you had not experienced before? Did it feel strange to chew 10-15 times?

## Cravings

Cravings usually occur when we have not eaten healthy foods that give us what our bodies need. When we crave, our bodies usually seek foods that are high in calories or fat in order to satisfy the void in our stomachs. An example of this would be if we are lacking minerals like zinc or magnesium, which are found in meats, we might crave a chocolate bar, which contains the same ingredients. Cravings are not reasons to eat. While they might be a reason to eat healthier and take necessary supplements, it is not a reason to eat. Many people confuse cravings as hunger. This leads to overeating and loading up on calories that result in weight gain.

An emotional craving is one in which no actual feelings of physical hunger exist. This type of hunger does not increase if you wait a few minutes or distract yourself. The underlying emotion behind your hunger will increase. Emotional cravings are reduced when your emotion is addressed. Common emotional triggers of craving are: stress, anxiety, depression, loneliness, boredom, sadness, anger, and PMS.

The American culture uses food for comfort and as a response to behavior. As children, we were raised to associate food with certain emotions. For example, you may have gotten a cookie for being good. Ice cream is the prescription food given after we get our tonsils out. Chicken soup is the food we request when we feel sick. It is necessary to break this association between certain comfort foods and emotional states of mind. It is important to make a distinction between your emotional state and food in order to effectively address and cope with the true problems in your life. Notice what your body is really craving. If you're just overtired, take a nap instead of reaching for that box of cookies. Take a short walk or read something funny instead of eating cake when you feel sad or depressed. Take a multivitamin to make sure you're getting enough nutrients. Soak in a hot tub if you want to reward yourself. As a life long solution, feed the real void in your life instead of reaching for food.

## Avoid Cravings

Hunger can be held off by distractions. Cravings can be killed with distractions. Many times people eat out of boredom. Prepare for this experience by developing distractions. Distractions can be any activity that causes your brain to become engaged and disengaged from the thoughts of the food craving. Examples of distractions can be to read a book, work a puzzle, go for a walk, or reread your Reasons for Weight Loss card.

Delaying your cravings can help you avoid them. Here are some ideas to kill cravings.

- Eat healthy snacks to regulate your blood sugar levels.
- Take a multivitamin to meet your nutritional needs.
- Drink water.
- Take some deep breaths and do a quick visualization.
- Take a nap.
- Go for a short walk.
- Listen to music.

- Do not put food on a forbidden list. This makes your desire for them stronger. Eat them in MODERATION.
- Remind yourself that it is not 'all or nothing'. Eating one bad food will not be the end of your goals. Enjoy it and move on.

## Distractions List

Identify distractions that are realistic for you. List some easy distractions to use when you feel challenged to eat from cravings.

1.

2.

3.

4.

5.

6.

7.

8.

9.

10.

## Plan for Week 3

1) Read your Personal Goals and Positive Reprogramming cards daily.

2) Track yourself on your DFJ. Include food, activity, and positive thoughts.

3) Eat what you want, when you want. Stop eating
when you begin to feel full.

4) Sit down to eat EVERYTHING. Put you fork or
spoon down between each bite. Eat slowly and
pay attention to the taste and texture of the food
to increase your satisfaction and allow your
brain to register that you are full to avoid overeating.

5) Complete the savor the food exercise to teach
and use the experience to assist your new slower
paced eating plan.

6) Make a list of Distractions to use to avoid snacking and cravings.

7) Start taking a multivitamin.

**Weekly Check In**

Date:

Current Weight:                Goal Weight:

Measurements:

Arm_____    Stomach_____    Thigh_____



BMI:                           Goal BMI:

# Reprogram Yourself to Think Thin

The significant problems we face cannot be solved
by the by the same level of thinking that created them.
**Albert Einstein**

I am sure that you have heard the phrase,
thoughts create things. Essentially what you focus on,
good or bad, you attract into your life because your
subconscious is hard at work to align your life with
your beliefs. This is also called the Law of Attraction.
Can you think of some recent events you have experienced that you expected and/or anticipated? Have you
been really worried that something would happen and
then it happened? I am guessing that you can think of
several examples in your life or someone else's life.
These are no coincidences. What you focus on grows in
your life. This can occur quickly or over time, but it
does in fact occur. If you are not happy with the results
that you have achieved so far, read on for several ways
to reprogram your brain for different results.

Your thoughts drive your behaviors, your reactions to events, your awareness of opportunity, and
your decisions. Regardless of your beliefs, you will be
more aware of the environmental experiences that
support your belief. What you think about, you bring
about. When people train as race car drivers, they are
taught to keep their eyes focused on the path they want
to drive especially if they spin or loose control of the
car. This focus on the track keeps their subconscious
directing their brain to focus on driving on the track to
keep them from hitting the wall in these dangerous
situations.

In the U.S., sport psychology has been used to correct problems. In the former Soviet Union, sport psychology concentrated on creating methods to maximize performance. In one experiment, four matched groups of world class Soviet athletes trained before the 1980 Winter Games at Lake Placid, as follows:

Group I- 100% Physical Training
Group II- 75% Physical Training, 25% Mental
Group III- 50% Physical Training, 50% Mental
Group IV- 25% Physical Training, 75% Mental

Which group showed the greatest improvement? Group IV. (Garfield and Bennett, 1989)

Thoughts create visualizations that create your reality. These athletes spent more time mentally rehearsing then physically rehearsing. This is a strong support for the power of your visualizations. What are you visualizing? Have you been allowing your mind to remain on default settings without editing for your goals? Are you visualizing your success or replaying your failures? Are you visualizing your skinny self or do you constantly think about being fat?

I am not suggesting that you can think yourself thin without any other assistance. Simply thinking thin will not magically shrink your body overnight. You will need to add action to these thoughts. Your thin thoughts coupled with appropriate action can greatly assist your weight loss tremendously and create long term results. Thinking thin can create more positive food choices. Thin thoughts will help you develop an interest in an increased level of activity. You will be more open and interested in physical activity. Focusing on your Thin Thoughts will probably lead you to the gym or the track where other Thin Thinkers hang out. Thin thoughts are also likely to spark conversations with these like minded people. These people may become new friends that are supportive and empowering to your new goals.

- What are your thoughts about weight loss?
- Do you have confidence in yourself to lose weight?
- Do you feel that you have to be deprived to lose weight and keep it off long term?

Live out of your imagination, not your history.
**Stephen Covey**

## Create Your Reality

At this point you have most likely become more aware of the thoughts that have held you back in the past. You are addressing these sabotaging thoughts and creating motivation through positive interpretations of these negative thoughts that will certainly propel you toward your goals at a higher rate of speed than you have ever experienced in the past. Now I would like you to take your mental game to the next level.

I have already helped you to identify that your thoughts create your reality. If your mindset is focused on what you don't want to occur, you are subconsciously reacting to the opportunities to make this negative focus your reality and reinforce what you believe to be true. It is time to begin focusing on the positive goals that you want to happen. This starts with identifying specific goals and regularly reinforcing them. To some extent I have already gotten you started on this mission with the creation of your Reasons for Weight Loss cards and Positivity cards. The following three strategies will help you focus and reinforce your consistent visualization of your personal weight goals.

## I. Written Goals

There are thousands of books that discuss the importance of written goals. Written goals allow you to be clear on where you are going and to know when you arrive at your destination. A very small book that I recommend and personally reread regularly is titled It Works, by RHJ. This tiny 28 page gem gives the goal achieving formula to you in a nutshell that I will share with you here.

Write down your specific goals in order of importance. Write specific detail including goal dates. Write these goals using 'I am' statements as if the goals have already been achieved. Add reference to time. For example, 'It is January 1, 2009 and I am...' Read this list three times per day: morning, noon, and night. Think of these goals as achieved as often as possible. Visualize your goals as if you have achieved them when you read or think about them. What does your body look like? How do you feel?

Do not talk about your goals to anyone other than your higher power and your coach. Well meaning and some not so well meaning people in your life will be quick to share their opinions of your goals and your ability to achieve them. This will only add undo stress to your weight loss process. It is fine for everyone to know that you are working toward a healthier lifestyle. I am not intending you to be an undercover dieter. However, the details of your personal weight loss and image goals are personal to you. Outside influence can be discouraging and un-motivating which is completely unnecessary.

Some of these goals may be very similar to your Reasons for Weight Loss. Since you are a few weeks into the program, your personal goals may be a modification of your original Reasons for Weight Loss. If they are the same, keep using your existing cards. If you have reworked them in any way, update your cards for daily reading.

## Personal Goals

1.

2.

3.

4.

5.

6.

7.

8.

It is important to keep your personal goals updated. As you lose weight and maintain weight loss, you will begin to open yourself up to new experiences. Each year your body becomes healthier energizing you to strengthen your commitment to fun physical activities. If you start your exercise regimen with walking, you may eventually start running and later develop a desire to complete a marathon. Maybe you start taking Tae Kwon Do and develop a desire to work toward a black belt. Each year you may have exciting new goals to accomplish. You may revisit this exercise each year to keep a focus on the current goals you set for yourself. The reinforcement goal cards that you create for yourself work for any goal you set for yourself.

## II. Vision Board

Vision Boards are very effective and a lot of fun. While you can use this idea for any goal you develop, we are going to create a vision board totally related to your weight loss goals. This board will be a pictorial reminder of your goals and solicit an emotional response which assists in elevating your motivation to stay the course you have begun.

A vision board is much like a collage that is meant to reinforce your goals. You can choose a poster paper, cork board or large empty picture frame to get started. Select pictures or text to represent your goals as achieved. Fill your poster or board with a variety of images that represent your goals and make you feel good when you look at it. You may take a picture of yourself and modify it with a computer photo program to look like your slimmer self. You may have older pictures of yourself at your ideal weight. Add pictures of clothing in the sizes that you will be wearing. You may add a written statement that say's 'I am a size __'.

Here are some other ideas to get you creative:
- Picture of a scale with your goal weight in the window
- Pictures of activities that you will be engaged in doing
- Pictures of places that you will be visiting (i.e. your kid's sports games, certain stores that offer the clothes you will wear, the beach)

- Pictures of clothing you will wear with the size tag showing your new clothing size
- Text that states one of your affirmations
- A copy of your drivers license with the weight changed to reflect your goal weight
- Picture of a body size that matches your goal with your face pasted on the head

Fill your board with multiple images and make sure that each of these images makes you feel good when you think about your thin self in these pictures. Add pictures as you find or think of more pictures to add. Hang or post this board where you will see it daily. Your bathroom is a great place for your vision board because it is private and you will be in that room everyday. Hanging by the bathroom sink is great because you are sure to look at it daily while you brush your teeth. It is important that you take time everyday to focus on your board and imagine these images to be true for you in the moment.

Use this focused time to continue to reprogram your mind for thin thinking. As you look at your thin images, tell yourself that you look good. Focus on the end result of your slim physique and do not think about how you achieve it. Tell yourself that you are thin. You may not feel thin and this might feel silly, however, you will need to reprogram your thinking about your body image. You have to replace all the negative thoughts that you routinely think. It is no surprise that replacing these thoughts will feel funny or awkward at first. It is ok if you giggle when you look at and let yourself feel the experience of your vision board, your mind will receive the messages over time and believe this new truth about yourself. As you start believing that you look good and anticipating your new slim figure, you will be more energized to seek out positive ways to achieve the goal. You might find that this mental picture of your slim body flashes in your mind when you find yourself in a food tempting situation helping you to avoid the temptation. Nothing tastes better than skinny feels. By focusing on the result, your mind will create the plan of action over time.

*III. Visualization through Relaxation*
This technique will be covered in the following chapter.

## Plan for Week 4

1) Read your Reasons for Weight Loss/Positive reprogramming cards daily before each meal and for a motivation boost. Keep a small copy in your wallet so that you have this motivation boost at all times to use to distract from cravings.

2) Track yourself on your DFJ: food, activity, positivity.

3) Eat what you want when you are hungry and STOP eating when you begin to feel full.

4) Sit down to eat EVERYTHING. Eat slowly and put utensils down between each bite. Pay attention to the taste and texture of the food to increase your satisfaction and allow your brain to register that you are full to avoid overeating.

5) Use your list of Distractions to prepare your plan to avoid snacking and cravings. Use these distractions to avoid eating due to hunger when it is not the appropriate time to eat.

6) Write down your personal weight loss and image goals. Include emotion with the statements for increased effectiveness. Keep this personal.

7) Create your Vision Board and hang it up in your home. Spend at least 5 to 10 minutes each day focusing on your Vision Board. Let yourself feel what these images will feel like when they are a reality in your life.

---

## Weekly Check In

Date:

Current Weight:            Goal Weight:

Measurements:

Arm_____     Stomach_____     Thigh_____

BMI:                       Goal BMI:

# Visualize Your Ideal Self

Imagination is everything.
It is the preview to life's coming attractions.
**Albert Einstein**

## Create Your Reality

The first two strategies to help you focus and reinforce your consistent visualization of your personal weight goals were covered in the previous chapter. This is the third and very important strategy.

### III. Visualization through Relaxation

Visualization and Relaxation has long been proven to assist people in lowering their blood pressure, modifying a mood, and reducing pain. Heart patients and chronic pain patients are taught this skill to improve their health. The relaxation technique, Visualization, can be used to reinforce your goals much like the written list and vision board.

Researchers have found that when you perform real life tasks, your brain uses the identical processes it would use if you were only vividly visualizing or mentally rehearsing the task. In a 1992 study, Anne Isaac examined the effectiveness of mental practice on sports skills. Seventy eight subjects participated. Subjects were divided into two groups. One group had no intervention to their regular practice schedule. The experimental group utilized visualization or mental practice for three specific trampoline skills. Training lasted six weeks. The experimental group showed significantly more improvement. (Isaac, 1992) Jack Nicklaus, the highly acclaimed and accomplished professional golfer said, "I never hit a shot without having a very sharp, in-focus picture of it in my head. It's like a color

movie." Visualizing yourself achieving your goal sets
the action in motion to make this a reality. Visualization or mental rehearsal is a standard in peak sports
performance. This technique will work with the same
effectiveness for your weight loss process.
Repetitive visualization of your completed goals
is important because it creates a conflict with your
subconscious mind between what you are visualizing
and your current status. Your subconscious mind tries
to resolve that conflict by turning your current reality
into the new vision. It programs the Reticular Activating System (RAS) in your brain to start letting into
your awareness anything that will help you achieve
your goals. I know that sounds a little scientific, but
stay with me. Visualization activates your subconscious to create solutions to make your goal a reality
and it creates motivation. This concept translated into
English is: Life is Mental. Take control of your life
when you are ready!

The reticular activating system is defined by
Wikipedia as the part of the brain believed to be the
center of arousal and motivation. Your reticular activating system is like a filter between your conscious
mind and your subconscious mind. Your conscious
mind gives your RAS instructions and it and passes
them on to your subconscious. The RAS filters out
millions of bits of information from your environment
so that you are not overwhelmed. Only information
necessary for your survival or information to assist in
achieving your goals is let through your conscious mind
to your subconscious mind. For example, your instruc-
tion to your conscious is "listen for my friend saying my
name". In a noisy crowd, if you are looking for your
friend, you will be able to hear your friend calling your

name. Your RAS filters out the noise to let through the sound of your friend calling your name.

You can program your conscious mind by giving it specific instructions necessary to achieve your goals. This is why developing thin thinking works. Daily reading of your personal goal cards (affirmations) is an example of programming and instructing your conscious mind. Your RAS is literal and cannot distinguish between 'real' or 'imagined' events. This explains why visualization is an effective way to program your RAS. Visualize yourself at your goal weight and your RAS thinks this is a truth. It then filters information to your subconscious to support the image. Daily use of both your affirmation cards and visualizing your goal as achieved reprograms your mind to create this reality. This is thin thinking.

Because your RAS is literal, focus only on what you want to occur. It does not understand negatives. Your RAS cannot distinguish between 'want' and 'do not want'. Visualizing 'not' eating an entire cake is the same as being focused on eating cake. There is no visual or picture for 'not' eating cake. The only visual is of the cake, so your subconscious receives the message to eat cake. This visualization or thought will most likely provoke a craving for cake. This explains why worrying about something that you do not want to happen actually assists in creating your concern. You focus on what you are worried about and you have a vivid visualization of what you do not want to happen. This attention to your worry visualization tells the RAS to filter for information to match it and your subconscious sets out to make it a reality. There is something to be said for the phrase "don't worry, be happy." So avoid visualizing what you 'do not' want, instead visualize what you 'do' want.

Visualizing the successful achievement of your goals establishes a mental rehearsal that your RAS believes to be a reality.   Create and practice a very specific visualization of your goal as already achieved and your RAS will pass it off to your subconscious which goes to work creating the visualization into a reality. Your subconscious works using pictures which you give it via the visualization.  The visualization assists the RAS in identifying the important environmental experiences that will assist you in achieving your goals.

Visualization works best when used as a relaxation exercise.  Your visualization should focus on happy and soothing images that create a relaxed response from your body.  Relaxation works best when you train your body to respond automatically.  To train your body, use this technique with consistency.  In other words, repeat the procedure the same way every time using your environment.  Find a comfortable chair or your bed for relaxation and use this spot each time you practice.  Use a candle or room spray with a scent that you feel is relaxing to you.  Your olfactory sense is very responsive to repetitious conditioning.  Find a radio station with relaxing music or use a soothing relaxation CD in the background as you relax.  Use the same or very similar music with each relaxation session.  You will find that your body will start becoming relaxed very quickly as you repeat these environmental cues.  It is as if your body recognizes the special music and says 'ok, start relaxing'.

If you are questioning me on this idea of developing an instant relaxation response, think about a smoker's behavior.  Smokers will many times smoke to relax.  They are using deep breathing with a cigarette to relax.  I am sure that you have watched a smoker smile as they put a cigarette to their lips and take long deep drags. Repetitive smoking associated with relaxation will create this relaxation memory for them just like the environmental triggers can for you. Ask a smoker if they start feeling relaxed just by pulling a cigarette out of the box. I am certain they will say yes. You can train yourself the same way without the cigarette.

To get started, write or think of a detailed description of your optimal self image as if your goals have been achieved. This may easily be developed from your list of personal goals. Include only the positive goals that you want to achieve. Do not include any negatives to avoid. Remember your RAS is literal and cannot distinguish between the pictures of goals and avoidances. Focus only on the goals you want to achieve. Create the visual of your thin self in a specific setting like the beach, or with friends in a social setting, etc. Use details for this visual that include your five senses: sight, smell, touch, taste and hearing. This will become your standard visualization for your evening practice. Visualization is very important to reaching your goal. Your subconscious is always at work to respond in accordance with your thoughts and beliefs. Visualization will help you focus on the goals that will illicit assistance from your subconscious. This skill will clarify your goal and set your subconscious on course to work with you on your journey.

*Master the Skill:*
Let yourself clearly visualize yourself in detail.
What size are your clothes?
What is your groomed appearance?
What does your hair look like?
How does your skin feel?

What do you smell like?
What activity are you enjoying?
What does the environment around you smell
like?
What textures are touching your skin?
What music or sounds are around you?

Daily practice of your visualization is important.
Choose the same relaxation spot with relaxing music
and a relaxing scent. One easy way to relax is to
practice when you have readied yourself for sleep, lie
comfortably in your bed and take a few deep breaths.
Deep breathing is achieved by breathing in through
your nose bringing the air down to your diaphragm and
making your belly expand. If your chest is moving but
not your belly, you are not breathing deeply. Release
the air slowly and completely through your mouth
making a whooshing sound. Repeat this 3 to 5 times.
Spend 5-10 minutes thinking about the details of your
optimal self image. The more evenings that you practice this visualization, the easier and more vivid the
visualization will become. Repetition will train you to
quickly experience the visualization at any time of day
in any setting. The more frequently you rehearse the
visualization the more effective this technique will be
for you.

## Modify Your Eating with Visualization

Visualization can be used to modify your eating
and food choices. You can create a food aversion to any
food that you tend to crave. This aversion allows you to
feel free of the cravings. Do you have any certain foods
that you eat in excess? Are sugary foods, chips and
other junk foods your downfall? Because your brain
cannot distinguish between real events and vividly

imagined events, you can use vivid visualization to modify your eating.

## Create a Food Aversion

Food aversions can be created for your benefit. This may be a little 'out of the box' for you, but it can be a very effective strategy. There are probably certain foods that you have an aversion to because it once made you sick or you do not like what it looks, smells or tastes like. The negative reaction that the food caused is probably still so vivid in your mind that they food is not desired. There may be certain foods that you would like to have an aversion to in order to avoid the calories. Maybe you have a weakness for candy, fried chicken, etc. If this is the case, spend some time thinking about this food to identify anything that you find disturbing to create an aversion. For example, I can easily kill my appetite at any 'serve yourself' food restaurant. If I let myself think about how many people may have touched the food with dirty hands or by recognizing that the sneeze guard is not adequate coverage, I cannot eat the food.

Even though my boys are almost four years apart, each of them experienced a self inflected food aversion stage around the age of five. My oldest son realized that a fried chicken leg was actually the leg of a chicken and would not eat chicken for months. My youngest son was fond of pigs and refused to eat sausage when he realized that pork sausage was once a pig. The knowledge of these food origins caused a food aversion for both boys for extended periods of time.

If you are struggling with a certain food that you cannot identify an immediate aversion, then use visualization to create one. Vividly visualize the food you want to avoid. Create a strong visualization of yourself eating this food. Close your eyes and move your mouth like you are chewing this food. Notice the taste and texture of the food. Can you taste it? Now imagine adding worms to this visualization or dust from the corners of a public place and keep chewing with this new addition to your mouth. How does the food taste now with this nasty addition? Can you taste the grit from the dust and the worms? The point of this is to make you feel disgusted. Focus on the textures and smells as you chew. What does it feel like on your tongue? What does it feel like as you swallow? Keep chewing with your favorite food in the nasty mix. It is important that you physically feel the food in your mouth to create this food aversion trigger. As you vividly visualize chewing your favorite food with a nasty mix, squeeze your thumb and middle finger on your left hand together and keep them squeezed. Keep the visualization experience and the squeezing for a minute or two. You are creating a negative association with the food you crave by the action with your fingers. The more vivid your visualization is, the more intense the food aversion. Now at any time, you can again squeeze your left thumb and middle finger together to illicit this queasy feeling to avoid the craving or food. Any time you feel the craving you want to avoid, squeeze your left thumb and middle finger together.

This is a very effective way to avoid cravings and certain foods. You will need to repeat the exercise to strengthen the trigger as you get started. The more vividly you experience the visualization, the stronger your trigger. Make certain that you feel the physical experience of chewing when you set the trigger. After repetitive use over time, you will need to repeat the exercise again to strengthen the trigger for effectiveness.

## Create a Mood Stabilizer

Many times the food you crave is a really a mood stabilizer of some sort. Maybe you eat chocolate when you feel depressed or bored. You can use a visualization to stabilize your mood instead of turning to food. Instead of eating to feel better, you use a trigger that you create. You will create a positive trigger much like you created the negative trigger only this time use your right thumb and forefinger. Think about when you have felt your best. This may be a past experience that you felt fabulous. You were happy, energetic and self confident. As you think about this memory, make it colorful and notice the textures around you. Create this visualization to be as vivid as you can make it. Physically experience the visualization. Maybe your breathing changes, your posture improves or you feel yourself doing a certain activity. When the visualization becomes vivid and you can feel it in your body, squeeze your right thumb and middle finger together and hold it. Keep squeezing while you focus on and fully experience your vivid visualization. This is creating a positive association that can be used anytime you want to feel good. If you feel depressed or bored and start thinking about eating, squeeze your right thumb and forefinger together to elicit the positive response. Repeat the exercise to strengthen your trigger. Over time, you will need to reprogram your triggers by completing the visualization and the squeeze process.

## Plan for Week 5

1) Read and visualize your Personal Goals and Positive Reprogramming cards daily. Post in your home and wallet.

2) Track yourself on your DFJ: food, activity, positivity.

3) Use your Reasons for Weight Loss to overcome challenges and motivate you.

4) Eat when you are hungry and stop eating when you begin to feel full.

5) Sit down to eat EVERYTHING. Eat slowly and put utensils down between bites. Pay attention to the taste and texture of the food to increase your satisfaction and allow your brain to register that you are full to avoid overeating.

6) Use your list of Distractions to avoid snacking and cravings. Use these distractions to avoid eating due to hunger when it is not the appropriate time to eat.

7) Focus attention on your vision board at least once a day.

8) Spend 5-10 minutes each evening doing the visualization of your optimal self image. Create a new nightly habit with this exercise. As you become proficient with this skill, think about your visualization at any opportunity possible.

9) Create a food aversion and a mood stabilizer. Use these triggers during the week to avoid your craved food and to uplift your mood.

---

**Weekly Check In**

Date:

Current Weight:            Goal Weight:

Measurements:

Arm_____        Stomach_____        Thigh_____


BMI:                              Goal BMI:

---

# Practical Strategies for Challenges

Week six and you are surely making progress at this point. We have your thinking on track for your goals and positively focused for long term results. This week will focus on several behavioral techniques to help you overcome food challenges. These are straightforward practical solutions to everyday food challenges.

## Cue Control Eating

Cue control eating refers to situations (cues) that encourage unnecessary or unhealthy eating. Review your DFJ and identify any situations that encourage unnecessary eating. Are you snacking in front on the TV? If so, turn off the TV and read a book or put snacks in a small bowl and eat them slowly without refilling. Are you going to restaurants that too tempting to keep on track with your healthy food choices? If so, avoid this restaurant until you feel stronger in sticking to your food plan. Do you overeat or make poor food choices with certain friends? Avoid involving food when visiting with these friends. Create a solution as you identify these patterns. Avoid these situations, change the setting or sever the relationships between the situation and food.

Use the cue controlled behavior to your advantage. Start creating positive cues for yourself. Create healthy snack alternatives for cue control food challenges like going to the movies, attending sporting events, etc. Essentially you are creating a positive new food replacement habit instead of restricting/denying yourself. If you identify a certain time of day or activity (like watching TV) that challenge you sticking to your calorie plan, prepare for the challenge. Eat a healthy snack before this time of day to avoid hunger. Plan and prepare a healthy snack to enjoy during this time of day. Replace your standard poor food choices with healthy positive food choices. For example, if you eat potato chips while watching television, eat pickle slices instead of chips. Replace a bad habit with a good habit. It is much easier to modify your behaviors than to try to avoid them all together. When you modify or replace a behavior with a better alternative, you will not feel that you are depriving yourself.

## Do Not Go Cold Turkey

The thought of dieting or modifying your eating habits can send a chill of despair down your spine. You may have a history or restricting yourself so much that you set yourself up for failure. Not this time. As you identify your food challenges according to food, time of day or activity; develop a solution. Plan to eat only a small amount of the poor food choice. Allowing yourself to eat your candy bar, cookies or pie in small amounts regularly will keep you from feeling deprived and wanting to binge.

## Portion Control

To minimize the temptation of second and third helpings when eating at home, serve the food on individual plates, instead of putting the serving dishes on the table. Make only what your family will eat. Keeping the excess food out of reach and out of sight may discourage overeating. If you make excess, put the excess away immediately.

## TV Treats

When eating or snacking in front of the TV, put the amount that you plan to eat into a bowl or container instead of eating straight from the package. It's easy to overeat when your attention is focused on something else. If eating while watching TV is a challenge that frequently leads to excess or unnecessary eating, you might decide not to eat at all while watching TV.

## Out of Sight, Out of Mind

People tend to consume more when they have easy access to food. Make your home a "portion friendly zone."

- Replace the candy dish with a fruit bowl.
- If you need to purchase tempting foods, like cookies, chips, or ice cream. Store them out of immediate eyesight, like on a high shelf or at the back of the freezer. Move the healthier food to the front at eye level.
- When buying in bulk, store the excess in a place that's not convenient to get to, such as a high cabinet or at the back of the pantry.

## Be Aware of Large Packages

The larger the package, the more people consume from it without realizing it. To minimize this effect:

- Divide up the contents of one large package into several smaller containers to help avoid over-consumption.
- Don't eat straight from the package. Instead, serve the food in a small bowl or container.

## Use Smaller Plates

This is a simple idea with a big impact. If you are using very large plates and bowls for food, you might want to make a change.

These large pieces may look pretty for the food presentation, but the temptation to eat large portion sizes is intense. Try using these large pieces with healthy portion sizes and you will think you are eating elf food. That is no way to start a meal. Looking at elf food before you start eating will convince yourself that you will be left hungry. Using smaller plates helps you transition to healthier portions without visually feeling like you are missing something. The smaller plates will make the healthy portion sizes look abundant.

## Kitchen is Closed Two Hours Before Sleep

Eating three healthy meals with two healthy snacks will give you all the necessary calories daily. Make certain that your final meal is at least two hours before you go to sleep. These two hours are necessary for your metabolism to effectively burn calories. Your body may be more likely to store your late night snack as fat with a slower night time metabolism.

## Treat Yourself

When you choose to treat yourself with a food that is not part of your daily plan like chips or ice cream, keep your serving size to the minimum. Savor the experience by eating slowly and enjoying the experience. It is important to allow yourself to enjoy these little treats at different times. This keeps you from feeling food deprived. You can eat whatever you choose. Just remind yourself that regularly choosing healthy food will keep you thin.

## Give Yourself Credit

When you feel challenged, focus on the positive progress that you have made to date. Be sure to include the small steps of progress. If you were boating across a large lake, you would focus on crossing the lake and arriving at your destination. You would need to look behind you to judge how far you had gone and estimate your time of arrival. Life is no different. Read over the DFJ entries and look back at where you were just three weeks ago and identify all the new techniques you have developed and physical progress you have made. Your thoughts are growing more positive. Your visualization is improving in clarity. You have most likely avoided several temptations. There are many more things credit worthy in your life to identify. Jot these down on your DFJ in your positivity entries as you think of them. Reading back over these credits as you move forward will boost your motivation and create more credit to acknowledge.

## Mental Flexibility

You are developing your physical flexibility through your exercise regime; now let's build your mental flexibility. Many times when people begin losing weight there is a hiccup in the program. Late night snacking or a fatty food splurge can send you into a tailspin with guilt and remorse. No guilt and remorse for you! If you start thinking that you have blown your program, stop that thought! Thin people do not think those kinds of thoughts. They are mentally flexible. Thin people adjust their eating **slightly** after a splurge to accommodate. They enjoy their splurge and then get back to their normal eating habits. This does not mean starve yourself the day after you splurged. That would send your body into fat storage mode. Simply eat your daily calories as planned choosing the healthiest food options possible. If you splurge, enjoy the experience and then pull out your Personal Goals card and your Reasons for Weight Loss card to get back on track.

## Plan for Week 6

1) Read your Personal Goals and Positive Reprogramming cards daily posted in your home and wallet.

2) Track yourself on your DFJ. Include food, activity, positivity and daily credits.

3) Eat when you are hungry and stop eating when you begin to feel full.

4) Sit down to eat EVERYTHING. Eat slowly and put utensils down between bites. Pay attention to the taste and texture of the food to increase your satisfaction and allow your brain to register that you are full to avoid overeating.

5) Use your list of Distractions to avoid snacking and cravings. Use these distractions to avoid eating due to hunger when it is not the appropriate time to eat.

6) Spend 5-10 minutes each evening doing the visualization of your optimal self image.

7) Use your food aversion and mood stabilizing triggers.

8) Review your DFJ to indentify food challenges associated with environmental cues. Develop solutions to end the relationship between these cues and eating.

---

**Weekly Check In**

Date:

Current Weight:                    Goal Weight:

Measurements:

Arm_____      Stomach_____      Thigh_____



BMI:                               Goal BMI:

# Healthy Eating

"Discipline is the bridge between goals and accomplishments."
**Jim Rohn**

Healthy eating involves healthy food choices and portion sizes that match the serving size appropriate for your calorie intake goals. A portion is the amount of food you choose to eat. This may be the serving of food you put on your plate or the amount of food pre packaged. The serving size is identified on the back of the food package in the nutritional fact chart. The nutritional fact chart will indicate the amount of calories, fats, sodium, etc in each serving size to help you identify how many servings are appropriate. Most food is not packaged in individual serving sizes. Make sure you read the label to decide how much to eat.

The 'Value Meal' deals have made it more challenging to identify a healthy portion. For just a few cents more, the value meal will increase your portions significantly. Is that a great deal or what? The answer is 'or what'. For a few cents more, you just increased the size of your thighs, stomach and most likely your bottom! Many fast food restaurants are offering healthier options like fruit instead of fries. Take advantage of the healthy option as you drive through. If you treat yourself to fries, order the smallest portion available.

Developing a sense for healthy portion sizes is important. While many resources are available to educate yourself on portion sizes, the WIN publication from the National Institutes of Health (NIH Publication No. 03-5287) offers these great practical tips for recognizing serving sizes using everyday objects.

Visualize these everyday objects to judge serving sizes easily.

| Serving Sizes | Everyday Objects |
|---|---|
| ¼ raisins | one large egg |
| 3 ozs of meat/poultry | deck of cards |
| 1 cup of cereal | your fist |
| ½ cup of rice or pasta | half of a baseball |
| 1 baked potato | your fist |
| 1 medium fruit | a baseball |
| ½ cup of fresh fruit | ½ baseball |
| 1 ½ ozs low fat/fat free cheese | 4 stacked dice |
| ½ cup of ice cream | ½ baseball |
| 2 tbs peanut butter | a ping pong ball |

According to the WIN publication, the more frequently you eat out, the more body fat you will acquire. In a restaurant setting, you are more likely to eat larger portions and eat beyond your fullness signal. The following behavioral techniques will assist you in keeping your portion sizes healthy when you are eating out.

**Successfully Eating Out**
Restaurant portion sizes have gotten larger in the last few years. The trend has also spilled over into the grocery store, where a bagel are now supersized and the individual size bag of chips are double what they used to be. Research shows that people unintentionally consume more calories when faced with larger portions. This can mean a significant increase to calorie intake. Here are some tips to help you avoid some common portion-size pitfalls.

## Portion Control When Eating Out

Restaurants serve more food than one person needs at one meal. This contributes to overeating. Many people were told as children to eat everything on their plate. If this is you, it may be challenging for you to leave the over portioned food on your plate. It is time to reverse this mistaken directive. As an adult if you are still eating everything on your plate especially when eating out or eating a drive through Value Meal, change this thinking immediately. Take control of the amount of food that ends up on your plate.

✓ Share the dish with a friend.

✓ Ask for half of the dish to be boxed in carry out before your plate arrives at the table.

✓ Scoot the overflow portions to the edges of the plate and contaminate them by sprinkling sugar, salt and pepper to avoid eating them.

From the time that my husband and I dated, we have always shared one meal at restaurants. Not because we could not afford two meals, we shared one meal because we like to eat opposite things on the plate. One meal worked for both our appetites. This practice sometimes creates strange looks from the wait staff. At one restaurant years ago, the waiter offered to buy me another meal so that I had enough to eat. I laughed, my husband did not. This practice continues in our family with our three children. We strategize what to order to feed everyone without significant excess. Sharing meals is a very effective way to eat out and not blow your calorie intake. Ignore the strange looks and enjoy a slim body with a slim check!

## Swallow Before Reloading

Remember to eat consciously to keep your from plowing through a large portion. Put down utensils between bites. Chew your food slowly and savor every bite. This will lend itself to allowing you to feel full without overeating. As you eat each bite of food, do not put another bite of food on your fork or spoon until you have swallowed what is in your mouth. If your fork or spoon is not immediately loaded, you will be able to slow your eating. Put your fork or spoon on the table while chewing to avoid the temptation of reloading with food. You will recognize your full signal and stop eating appropriately.

## Do Not Eat Everything on Your Plate

Get realistic about the incorrect notion that you need to eat everything on your plate. This directive may have come from well meaning parents or care givers that wanted to be sure you were adequately nourished. You might have been told that because there are starving people in other parts of the world, you

"Don't give me the price of the specials, give me the calorie count."

need to appreciate your food and eat it all without waste. I have yet to have someone explain to me how eating everything on my plate will positively affect or feed people starving in other countries. Regardless of where you learned the concept, it is an irrational idea.

## Avoid Buffet Restaurants

I am convinced that buffet restaurants are the devil. While I say this tongue in cheek, I do believe that buffet restaurants are probably one of the most challenging environments for everyone. Cheap people like me feel the need to eat as much as possible to get their money's worth. Big eaters enjoy the multiple returns to the buffet to sample all foods and desserts offered. Both people leave feeling miserable.

On a business trip with my sister, Karen, we stopped for lunch at a Chinese buffet before our afternoon appointment. We ate and enjoyed a large variety of food. Karen mentioned that she was feeling full but had to try just a few more items. Soon I began giggling as I noticed that she had popped her buttons off her shirt. The more we laughed, the harder it was for her to try to pull her shirt back together. Apparently, she had left home that morning wearing a button down shirt that was bit snug fitting. Her multiple returns to the buffet could not be contained in that snug shirt and 'Bang' the buttons popped off. The money she spent buying a new shirt was more than what she saved on the buffet lunch. Do not let your local buffet bust off your buttons. Buffet's are a good example of restaurants to avoid.

## Go Ahead, Spoil Your Dinner

We learned as children not to snack before a meal for fear of "spoiling our dinner." Well, it's time to forget that old rule. If you feel hungry between meals, eat a healthy snack, like a piece of fruit or small salad, to avoid overeating during your next meal. Two small healthy snacks between meals will keep your meal portion smaller. Keep in mind this is not a license to eat at the slightest feeling of hunger. This is a strategy to avoid getting so hungry that you over eat at your next meal. Eating a healthy snack before dinner will also help you avoid overeating at a restaurant.

## Plan for Week 7
1) Read your Personal Goals and Positive Reprogramming cards daily posted in your home and wallet.

2) Track yourself on your DFJ. Include food, activity, positivity and daily credits.

3) Eat when you are hungry and stop eating when you begin to feel full.

4) Sit down to eat EVERYTHING. Eat slowly and put utensils down between bites. Pay attention to the taste and texture of the food to increase your satisfaction and allow your brain to register that you are full to avoid overeating.

5) Use your list of Distractions to avoid snacking and cravings. Use these distractions to avoid eating due to hunger when it is not the appropriate time to eat.

6) Spend 5-10 minutes each evening doing the visualization of your optimal self image.

7) Use your food aversion and mood stabilizing triggers. Reprogram their strength as needed over time.

8) Review your DFJ to indentify food challenges associated with environmental cues.  Develop solutions to end the relationship between these cues and eating.

9) Use behavioral techniques to handle public and private food challenges.

---

**Weekly Check In**

Date:

Current Weight:          Goal Weight:

Measurements:

Arm_____     Stomach_____     Thigh_____


BMI:                          Goal BMI:

# Reaching and Maintaining your Goal Weight

*Whatever you are ready for is ready for you.*

Congratulations for reaching the final week of your training. By this time, you have achieved your goals or you are well on your way to achieving your goals. This book can become your ongoing motivation to stay the course of thinking yourself thin. Your personal responses to the education and exercises in this book may change as you develop your thin thinking. That is an indicator of continued progress. This session focuses on several ways to maintain your successes and develop them further.

## Plateauing

Your weight will naturally plateau as you lose weight. A slow steady weight loss is healthiest and will result in a long term success because your body is adjusting as you lose weight. As you plateau, ask yourself if this weight is appropriate and healthy for you. If so, maintain your caloric intake and physical activity. If you plateau before reaching your goal weight and you would be healthier to lose more, increase your physical activity or restrict a small amount of calories a day. As your body adjusts to weight loss, it is normal for your body to require less calories. Reducing your calories by a small amount can start weight loss again.

## Say NO, Set Boundaries

Setting and keeping boundaries seems like an easy task, however, setting boundaries with 'food pushers' that you are emotionally connected to can be a

daunting task. There will be multiple situations in
your life that you will need to be strong and say 'no' to
food offerings.  Food pushers in your life may not be
malicious or mean spirited offering food that challenges
your thin  thinking.  These folks may simply be exercising what is believed to be good social skills by offering
an abundance of food (like at a celebration or holiday
meal that typically over indulges the guests in food).
When you say No to food in these settings or with
family gatherings, you are protecting your body.  Essentially you are saying No for self preservation.  When
these situations are uncomfortable or emotional, state
to the person, "Saying No is not about you, it is for me."
The other person can hear those words without feeling
hurt or defensive and you feel true to yourself.

## Mastermind for your Continued Success

Whether you have fully achieved your goal
weight or you are very close to your goal weight, continue to use the training from this education.  Hope-
fully the group dynamics have been helpful during the
first 8 weeks of your think thin journey.  Keep the
support going beyond this group.  Participate in your
coach's monthly maintenance groups.  Stay connected
with your group by creating an online group for members to communicate and offer continued support.  If
you have completed this training on your own, identify
people in your life that support your goals. Spend time
with these people regularly to keep revved up on the
boost you get from being around them.  Reread this
book over the next 8 weeks to ensure that you incorporate every piece of education into your daily life.  This
repetition will create the life change you desire. Use
this book as your continued reference to think thin for
life!

## Get a Life!

Broaden your horizons and develop personal interests. Maybe this means that your physical activity becomes a fun interest. Maybe you find new hobbies that you can now do with your new body. Keep yourself physical by joining a bike or run club, take martial arts, or join a sports league. Now is the time to try new things. These new things will keep you active and distract from a total focus on your weight. Managing weight loss is easier when you have a lot of other fun things going on in your life. Stay active, keep happy and think thin.

## Take 100% Responsibility for Your Weight

Take 100% responsibility for your life which includes your weight. Physical activity and food consumption is a choice. It is your choice. If you are able to take 100% responsibility for your life, you can make better choices.   You are the only person responsible for the quality of life you live. Do you take 100% responsibility for your life? Ask yourself these questions. Do you ever blame someone else for circumstances in your life? Do you ever complain about circumstances in your life? If you answered yes to either of these questions, you do not take full responsibility for your life. Being 100% responsible for your life means you understand that you create everything that happens to you. You take responsibility for your successes and failures. You have to give up blaming and give up complaining. Focus on your results. If you are unhappy with the results in your life, change your thoughts and your reactions to life experiences. Keep modifying your thoughts and reactions until you get the results you desire. No blaming, complaining or justifying. You choose it, you live it!

## Develop Responses to Triggers

This book has led you to identify various triggers in your life that affect your eating choices and patterns. Continue to look for patterns both productive and non productive. Eliminate the non productive patterns by using the cognitive strategies that you have learned. Enhance the productive patterns in the same way.

Seek out self help books that will encourage your personal growth. Commit to reading these books 30 minutes each day. This daily reading will enhance the skills that you have learned and develop you into a healthier person both mentally and physically. Filling your mind with positivity from these books daily will encourage continued healthy living choices. This small commitment can make a huge positive impact on your life.

## Plan for Week 8

Continue these action steps for weight maintenance.

1) Read your Personal Goals and Positive Reprogramming cards daily posted in your home and wallet.

2) Track yourself on your DFJ. Include food, activity, positivity and daily credits.

3) Eat when you are hungry and stop eating when you begin to feel full.

4) Sit down to eat EVERYTHING. Eat slowly and put utensils down between bites. Pay attention to the taste and texture of the food to increase your satisfaction and allow your brain to register that you are full to avoid overeating.

5) Use your list of Distractions to avoid snacking and cravings. Use these distractions to avoid eating due to hunger when it is not the appropriate time to eat.

6) Spend 5-10 minutes each evening doing the visualization of your optimal self image.

7) Use your food aversion and mood stabilizing triggers.

8) Review your DFJ to indentify food challenges associated with environmental cues. Develop solutions to end the relationship between these cues and eating.

9) Use behavioral techniques to handle public and private food challenges.

10) Take 100% responsibility for your life.

11) Commit to reading positive and educational books 30 minutes everyday.

## Weekly Check In

Date:

Current Weight:          Goal Weight:

Measurements:

Arm_____    Stomach_____    Thigh_____


BMI:                     Goal BMI:

# References

Stahre, L., & Hällström, T. (2005). A short-term cognitive group treatment program gives substantial weight reduction up to 18 months from the end of treatment. A randomized controlled trial. Eating and Weight Disorders, 10, 51-58.

Cooper, Z., Fairburn, C. G., & Hawker, D. M. (2003). Cognitive behavioral treatment of obesity: A clinician's guide. New York: Guilford Press.

Facing the Giants, by Kendrick, Alex and Kendrick, Stephen, Sherwood Pictures, 2006.

"A controlled trial of arthroscopic surgery for osteoarthritis of the knee" N Engl J Med 2002 Jul 11;347(2):81-8, Moseley JB; O'Malley K; Petersen NJ; Menke TJ; Brody BA; Kuykendall DH; Hollingsworth JC; Ashton CM; Wray NP
http://www.ncbi.nlm.nih.gov/entrez/query.fcgi?cmd=Retrieve&db=PubMed&list_uids=12110735

Peak Performance-Mental Training Techniques of the World's Greatest Athletes, by Charles A. Garfield and Hal Zina Bennett. New York: Warner Books, 1989.

It Works, by RHJ. California: DeVorss & Company, 1953.

Isaac, A. R. (1992). Mental Practice- Does it Work in the Field?, The Sport Psychologist, 6, 192-198.

"Just Enough for You about Food Portions," NIH Publication No. 03-5287, August 2006.

http://win.niddk.nih.gov/publications/just_enough.
htm

www.cartoonresources.com, HealthClub Cartoon

www.kazcartoonstore.com, Woman at Refrigerator
Cartoon

www.cartoonstock.com, Diet Dishes Cartoon

www.cartoonresources.com, Calorie Count Cartoon

# Appendix

Complete the Daily Food Journal forms to track your food intake, activity and exercise level and positivity. Be sure to include your daily self credits.

Date:

| Food Intake | | | | |
|---|---|---|---|---|
| Time | Place | Reason | Food | Amount |
| | | | | |

| Physical Activity | |
|---|---|
| Scheduled | |
| Spontaneous | |

| Positivity | |
|---|---|
| | |

Date:

**Food Intake**

| Time | Place | Reason | Food | Amount |
|------|-------|--------|------|--------|
|      |       |        |      |        |

**Physical Activity**

Scheduled

Spontaneous

Positivity

**Date:**

**Food Intake**

| Time | Place | Reason | Food | Amount |
| --- | --- | --- | --- | --- |
|  |  |  |  |  |

**Physical Activity**

Scheduled

Spontaneous

Positivity

**Date:**

**Food Intake**

| Time | Place | Reason | Food | Amount |
|------|-------|--------|------|--------|
|      |       |        |      |        |

**Physical Activity**

Scheduled

Spontaneous

**Positivity**

**Date:**

**Food Intake**

| Time | Place | Reason | Food | Amount |
|------|-------|--------|------|--------|
|      |       |        |      |        |

**Physical Activity**

Scheduled

Spontaneous

**Positivity**

Date:

**Food Intake**

| Time | Place | Reason | Food | Amount |
|------|-------|--------|------|--------|
|      |       |        |      |        |

**Physical Activity**

Scheduled

Spontaneous

**Positivity**

**Date:**

**Food Intake**

| Time | Place | Reason | Food | Amount |
|---|---|---|---|---|
| | | | | |

**Physical Activity**

Scheduled

Spontaneous

**Positivity**

Date:

**Food Intake**

| Time | Place | Reason | Food | Amount |
|---|---|---|---|---|
| | | | | |

**Physical Activity**

Scheduled

Spontaneous

**Positivity**

**Date:**

**Food Intake**

| Time | Place | Reason | Food | Amount |
|------|-------|--------|------|--------|
|      |       |        |      |        |

**Physical Activity**

Scheduled

Spontaneous

**Positivity**

Date:

## Food Intake

| Time | Place | Reason | Food | Amount |
|------|-------|--------|------|--------|
|      |       |        |      |        |

## Physical Activity

Scheduled

Spontaneous

## Positivity

**Date:**

## Food Intake

| Time | Place | Reason | Food | Amount |
|------|-------|--------|------|--------|
|      |       |        |      |        |
|      |       |        |      |        |

## Physical Activity

Scheduled

Spontaneous

## Positivity

Date:

**Food Intake**

| Time | Place | Reason | Food | Amount |
|---|---|---|---|---|
|  |  |  |  |  |

**Physical Activity**

Scheduled

Spontaneous

**Positivity**

**Date:**

**Food Intake**

| Time | Place | Reason | Food | Amount |
|------|-------|--------|------|--------|
|      |       |        |      |        |

**Physical Activity**

Scheduled

Spontaneous

Positivity

Date:

**Food Intake**

| Time | Place | Reason | Food | Amount |
|------|-------|--------|------|--------|
|      |       |        |      |        |

**Physical Activity**

Scheduled

Spontaneous

**Positivity**

**Date:**

**Food Intake**

| Time | Place | Reason | Food | Amount |
|---|---|---|---|---|
| | | | | |

**Physical Activity**

Scheduled

Spontaneous

Positivity

Date:

| Food Intake | | | | |
|---|---|---|---|---|
| Time | Place | Reason | Food | Amount |
| | | | | |

Physical Activity

Scheduled

Spontaneous

Positivity

**Date:**

**Food Intake**

| Time | Place | Reason | Food | Amount |
|------|-------|--------|------|--------|
|      |       |        |      |        |
|      |       |        |      |        |

**Physical Activity**

| Scheduled |  |
|-----------|--|
| Spontaneous |  |

**Positivity**

|  |
|--|

**Date:**

**Food Intake**

| Time | Place | Reason | Food | Amount |
|------|-------|--------|------|--------|
|      |       |        |      |        |

**Physical Activity**

Scheduled

Spontaneous

**Positivity**

**Date:**

**Food Intake**

| Time | Place | Reason | Food | Amount |
|------|-------|--------|------|--------|
|      |       |        |      |        |

**Physical Activity**

Scheduled

Spontaneous

**Positivity**

**Date:**

**Food Intake**

| Time | Place | Reason | Food | Amount |
|------|-------|--------|------|--------|
|      |       |        |      |        |
|      |       |        |      |        |

**Physical Activity**

Scheduled

Spontaneous

**Positivity**

Date:

**Food Intake**

| Time | Place | Reason | Food | Amount |
|------|-------|--------|------|--------|
|      |       |        |      |        |

**Physical Activity**

Scheduled

Spontaneous

Positivity

**Date:**

## Food Intake

| Time | Place | Reason | Food | Amount |
|---|---|---|---|---|
| | | | | |

## Physical Activity

| Scheduled | |
|---|---|
| Spontaneous | |

## Positivity

Date:

## Food Intake

| Time | Place | Reason | Food | Amount |
|------|-------|--------|------|--------|
|      |       |        |      |        |

## Physical Activity

Scheduled

Spontaneous

## Positivity

**Date:**

**Food Intake**

| Time | Place | Reason | Food | Amount |
|---|---|---|---|---|
|  |  |  |  |  |

**Physical Activity**

Scheduled

Spontaneous

**Positivity**

**Date:**

**Food Intake**

| Time | Place | Reason | Food | Amount |
|---|---|---|---|---|
| | | | | |

**Physical Activity**

| Scheduled | |
|---|---|
| Spontaneous | |

**Positivity**

| |
|---|

**Date:**

**Food Intake**

| Time | Place | Reason | Food | Amount |
|---|---|---|---|---|
|  |  |  |  |  |

**Physical Activity**

| Scheduled | |
|---|---|
| Spontaneous | |

**Positivity**

| |
|---|

**Date:**

**Food Intake**

| Time | Place | Reason | Food | Amount |
|------|-------|--------|------|--------|
|      |       |        |      |        |
|      |       |        |      |        |

**Physical Activity**

| Scheduled | |
|-----------|--|
| Spontaneous | |

**Positivity**

| | |
|--|--|

**Date:**

**Food Intake**

| Time | Place | Reason | Food | Amount |
|------|-------|--------|------|--------|
|      |       |        |      |        |
|      |       |        |      |        |

**Physical Activity**

| Scheduled |
|-----------|
|           |

| Spontaneous |
|-------------|
|             |

**Positivity**

|  |
|--|
|  |

**Date:**

**Food Intake**

| Time | Place | Reason | Food | Amount |
|---|---|---|---|---|
| | | | | |
| | | | | |

**Physical Activity**

Scheduled

Spontaneous

**Positivity**

Date:

**Food Intake**

| Time | Place | Reason | Food | Amount |
|------|-------|--------|------|--------|
|      |       |        |      |        |

**Physical Activity**

Scheduled

Spontaneous

**Positivity**

**Date:**

**Food Intake**

| Time | Place | Reason | Food | Amount |
|---|---|---|---|---|
| | | | | |

**Physical Activity**

Scheduled

Spontaneous

Positivity

Date: 

**Food Intake**

| Time | Place | Reason | Food | Amount |
|---|---|---|---|---|
| | | | | |

**Physical Activity**

Scheduled

Spontaneous

Positivity

Date:

**Food Intake**

| Time | Place | Reason | Food | Amount |
|------|-------|--------|------|--------|
|      |       |        |      |        |

**Physical Activity**

Scheduled

Spontaneous

Positivity

Date:

**Food Intake**

| Time | Place | Reason | Food | Amount |
|------|-------|--------|------|--------|
|      |       |        |      |        |
|      |       |        |      |        |

**Physical Activity**

Scheduled

Spontaneous

**Positivity**

**Date:**

**Food Intake**

| Time | Place | Reason | Food | Amount |
|---|---|---|---|---|
|  |  |  |  |  |

**Physical Activity**

| Scheduled |  |
|---|---|
| Spontaneous |  |

**Positivity**

|  |  |
|---|---|

Date:

**Food Intake**

| Time | Place | Reason | Food | Amount |
|---|---|---|---|---|
| | | | | |

**Physical Activity**

| Scheduled | |
|---|---|
| Spontaneous | |

**Positivity**

| |
|---|
| |

Date:

**Food Intake**

| Time | Place | Reason | Food | Amount |
|------|-------|--------|------|--------|
|      |       |        |      |        |

**Physical Activity**

Scheduled

Spontaneous

Positivity

Date:

**Food Intake**

| Time | Place | Reason | Food | Amount |
|------|-------|--------|------|--------|
|      |       |        |      |        |

**Physical Activity**

Scheduled

Spontaneous

Positivity

**Date:**

**Food Intake**

| Time | Place | Reason | Food | Amount |
|------|-------|--------|------|--------|
|      |       |        |      |        |

**Physical Activity**

Scheduled

Spontaneous

Positivity

Date:

**Food Intake**

| Time | Place | Reason | Food | Amount |
|------|-------|--------|------|--------|
|      |       |        |      |        |

**Physical Activity**

Scheduled

Spontaneous

Positivity

**Date:**

**Food Intake**

| Time | Place | Reason | Food | Amount |
|------|-------|--------|------|--------|
|      |       |        |      |        |

**Physical Activity**

Scheduled

Spontaneous

**Positivity**

**Date:**

**Food Intake**

| Time | Place | Reason | Food | Amount |
|------|-------|--------|------|--------|
|      |       |        |      |        |

**Physical Activity**

Scheduled

Spontaneous

**Positivity**

**Date:**

**Food Intake**

| Time | Place | Reason | Food | Amount |
|------|-------|--------|------|--------|
|      |       |        |      |        |

**Physical Activity**

Scheduled

Spontaneous

Positivity

**Date:**

**Food Intake**

| Time | Place | Reason | Food | Amount |
|------|-------|--------|------|--------|
|      |       |        |      |        |

**Physical Activity**

Scheduled

Spontaneous

Positivity

Date:

**Food Intake**

| Time | Place | Reason | Food | Amount |
|------|-------|--------|------|--------|
|      |       |        |      |        |

**Physical Activity**

Scheduled

Spontaneous

Positivity

Date:

**Food Intake**

| Time | Place | Reason | Food | Amount |
|------|-------|--------|------|--------|
|      |       |        |      |        |

**Physical Activity**

Scheduled

Spontaneous

Positivity

**Date:**

**Food Intake**

| Time | Place | Reason | Food | Amount |
|---|---|---|---|---|
|  |  |  |  |  |

**Physical Activity**

Scheduled

Spontaneous

**Positivity**

Date:

**Food Intake**

| Time | Place | Reason | Food | Amount |
|------|-------|--------|------|--------|
|      |       |        |      |        |

**Physical Activity**

| Scheduled |
|-----------|
|           |

| Spontaneous |
|-------------|
|             |

**Positivity**

|   |
|---|
|   |

**Date:**

**Food Intake**

| Time | Place | Reason | Food | Amount |
|------|-------|--------|------|--------|
|      |       |        |      |        |

**Physical Activity**

Scheduled

Spontaneous

**Positivity**

**Date:**

**Food Intake**

| Time | Place | Reason | Food | Amount |
|------|-------|--------|------|--------|
|      |       |        |      |        |
|      |       |        |      |        |

**Physical Activity**

| Scheduled |
|-----------|
|           |

| Spontaneous |
|-------------|
|             |

| Positivity |
|------------|
|            |

**Date:**

**Food Intake**

| Time | Place | Reason | Food | Amount |
|------|-------|--------|------|--------|
|      |       |        |      |        |

**Physical Activity**

Scheduled

Spontaneous

**Positivity**

**Date:**

**Food Intake**

| Time | Place | Reason | Food | Amount |
|------|-------|--------|------|--------|
|      |       |        |      |        |

**Physical Activity**

Scheduled

Spontaneous

**Positivity**

**Date:**

**Food Intake**

| Time | Place | Reason | Food | Amount |
|------|-------|--------|------|--------|
|      |       |        |      |        |

**Physical Activity**

Scheduled

Spontaneous

Positivity

**Date:**

**Food Intake**

| Time | Place | Reason | Food | Amount |
|------|-------|--------|------|--------|
|      |       |        |      |        |
|      |       |        |      |        |

**Physical Activity**

| Scheduled |
|-----------|
| Spontaneous |

**Positivity**

**Date:**

**Food Intake**

| Time | Place | Reason | Food | Amount |
|------|-------|--------|------|--------|
|      |       |        |      |        |

**Physical Activity**

Scheduled

Spontaneous

Positivity

**Date:**

**Food Intake**

| Time | Place | Reason | Food | Amount |
|------|-------|--------|------|--------|
|      |       |        |      |        |

**Physical Activity**

| Scheduled | |
|-----------|--|
| Spontaneous | |

**Positivity**

# About the Author

Kelly Stallings is a Licensed Professional Counselor with a Master's Degree in Counseling Psychology. She has more than 12 years of experience working with people in group settings to create significant changes in their life including increased overall physical health. Kelly has been married to her high school sweetheart for 20 years and they have three great kids. Kelly and her family 'Think Thin and Live Thin' in Texas.